Blues & Rock Harmonica Made Easy

By David Harp

Second Revised Edition

© 1993 Musical I. Press, Inc.
P.O. Box 1561
Montpelier, Vermont 05602

ISBN 0-918321-85-9

Book design by *Rita Ricketson*

Drawings by *Don Mayne*

Cover Photos by *Andrew Klein*

Acknowledgements:

Thanks to **Fred & Frieda** for letting me use the F & F Ranch to finish the manuscript, to **Wesleyan University** for teaching me how to write at the last possible minute, to **Tess** for her help, and to **Katie** and **Rita,** for everything...

Distributed to the music trade
by Music Sales Corporation

Distributed to the book trade
by Publishers Group West

Printed in the United States of America by
Vicks Lithographic and Printing Corporation

D1225784

A Few Other Books by David Harp

Instant Blues Harmonica (Volumes I and II)

Instant Chromatic Harmonica:
The Blues/Jazz Improvisation Method

Instant Guitar

Instant Flute

The Instant Harmonica Kit for Kids

Harmonica Positions Package

The Three Minute Meditator

Me and My Harmonica

Instant Blues/Rock Harmonica: The Video

Make Me Musical: Instant Harmonica, A Complete Musical Education for Kids

Metaphysical Fitness (with Dr. Nina Feldman)

The Three Minute Meditator Audiotape
(with Dr. Nina Feldman)

How To Whistle Like A Pro (with Jason Serinus)

Bending the Blues

EarthCards (with The Write for Action Group)

The New Three Minute Meditator

The Instant Rhythm Kit

In Hot Water: How To Save Your Back, Neck, and Shoulders In Ten Minutes A Day

How To Play Country & Western Harmonica

Music Theory Made Easy

Instant Harmonica for Kids: The Video

The Pocket Harmonica Songbook

Three Minutes to Blues Harmonica: The Video

Blues & Rock Harp Positions Made Easy (July 1996)

High & Fast Rock Harp Made Easy (August 1996)

Zen and the Art of Blues Harmonica (Nov. 1996)

How to Fight a Cold — And Win! (March 1996)

Contents

Read this First

After writing dozens of books and talking to many thousands of readers, I've found that — Big Surprise! — different people like to use my instructional methods in different ways. Some like to study every word, others like to skim to the "meat" of the method right away.

Some are experienced non-blues or rock players who need a bit of guidance, others are total harmonica beginners who need to be shown which end to blow into! Some would rather glance occasionally at a book while listening to a tape or viewing a video — others are exactly the opposite.

To please as many readers as possible, I've done two things. Firstly, for you viewer/listener types, I've created a video that can be used with this book, which you can read about on page 7. And secondly, I've developed **The Box System,** which I describe below. It will let you start playing right away. Then (when your lips need a break), you can come back and read about various harmonica issues in greater detail.

By the way: This book was created for **beginning** blues and rock harp players. It will get you playing some satisfying music right away, but it doesn't contain everything that you'll ever need to know.

In fact, I've tried to make sure that everything in this book can be completed by a beginner **within five to ten hours of practice** — a couple of long sessions, or a week or two's worth of shorter ones. And after you've finished this book, you'll be ready to go right on to the advanced beginner and intermediate material listed at the end of this book.

Using the Box System

If you're a total beginner, there's a certain amount of information that you really need to know before you even put your harmonica in your mouth. Plus, there's lots of other useful stuff that I'd like to tell you about, ranging from "Rhythm Harmonica" to "Licks and Fills". However, I also want to get you up and playing as soon as possible.

So I've put all of the really crucial beginning information into **boxes**, like this one.

If you want, you can read every word on every page, starting right now. But I'd advise you instead to skim through the pages and just read each box, look at any diagrams or pictures, and do the short exercises that I recommend. This will get you right into the "playing" part of the book, which begins on page 14.

Then, when your lips start to get tired from playing all the great stuff (and they will), **take a break!** Come back to the beginning of the book, and start reading the non-boxed sections that you skipped over, before. When your lips have recovered, play some more. Then take another break, and read some more unboxed sections.

By the time you've finished reading every word in the book, your lips will be in great shape, and you won't need "reading breaks" any more!

For you experienced players, the box system will get you to the more advanced material, right away. Since even lots of us good harpists never studied much music theory, you'll find that knowing the scales and chord structures will really help your playing!

What's in this Book?

There are three main things that this book will teach you. First, if you're a beginner, it will teach you everything you need to know about basic harmonica technique: How to hold it, how to blow it, and how to read my simple harmonica notation system.

Then it will teach you how to play what I call **"classic blues"** and **"classic rock"** music. The word "classic" simply refers to famous or popular songs or pieces of songs that have been written down, note for note. Just as every classical violin player should know certain famous pieces by Beethoven or Bach, every blues/rock harpist should know certain famous songs or "licks". What's a "lick"? I'll get around to that, soon!

Finally, this book will teach you to **improvise**, that is, to create your own blues and rock harmonica music as you go along.

After learning to play, some people find that they would mostly rather improvise, and others would mostly rather play "classics." But it's really good to know both of these exciting ways to make music.

Improvising is usually easier, at first, when you play along with other musicians. So if you decide that you want to do more improvising, you might try *Instant Blues Harmonica* (page 63), which teaches you how to create your own licks and solos and use them to jamm with the play-a-long cassette.

> First, this book will teach you **basic harmonica technique.** Then, it will teach you to play some **classic blues** and **rock songs** and **"licks"** that I've written down in simple harmonica notation. Finally, it will teach you to begin to **improvise**, that is, to create your own blues and rock harmonica music as you go along!

What's Not in this Book?

I don't mean to give you a "hard sell" here, but there's also a lot of important material that's not in this book. For instance, I wish that I had room for more about **improvising, more music theory,** more about **rhythm**, more **classic blues and rock licks,** and more about the incredibly useful technique known as **"bending"**. But if I had, this book would be close to 600 pages long, and only the larger libraries and universities could afford to buy one.

Fortunately (for me, at least, since it's how I make my living), I have put all of this information into other books, like *Instant Blues Harmonica, Music Theory Made Easy, The Instant Rhythm Kit, The Pocket Harmonica Songbook, Bending The Blues,* and many more. I'll mention these at appropriate places throughout this book, and describe each in greater detail in my sales pitch on pages 63 and 64.

About the Videocassette

If you like to learn by seeing and hearing, my video *Three Minutes to Blues Harmonica* (p. 63) covers most of what's in this book (plus more licks and solos), using my amazingly effective "Harmonica Hand Signal Method." It has lots of play-a-long music, too.

> If you like this book, and decide to keep on playing the harmonica, you may want to get some of my other books, tapes, and videos.

Solo or Accompanied

The humble "Tin Sandwich" or "Mississippi Saxo-phone" is an incredibly versatile and expressive instrument. It will fit in your pocket, and play beautiful hiking music far from the nearest electric outlet — that's called playing **solo.** Or it will perfectly complement a full blues band, or even an orchestra — that's **accompanied** harmonica.

Any song or piece of music will sound fine either played **solo** (harmonica, by itself) or with **accompaniment** (that is, along with other instruments).

However, I'll tell you if a particular song will really sound best played one way or the other.

An easy way to find some accompaniment is to use the one of my cassette or video methods (pages 63 - 63), unless you're lucky enough to have a guitar or keyboard playing friend.*

* If you don't, get a copy of *Instant Guitar* (page 63), and **create** your own jamming partner!

Four Main Ways to Play

There are four main ways in which a har-monica player can play — or play along with — blues and rock music: **Lead, Melody, Rhythm,** and **Fill** (also called **"lick"**) har-monica. Each way of playing will be explained and demonstrated in this book, and on the cassette. Usually, more than one of these ways (and sometimes even all four) are used by a harpist within a single song. They can all be played either solo or accompanied. If you like, you can read about them, right now, below.

Lead Harmonica

Lead (rhymes with "feed") harmonica players fill in the same role as a lead guitarist — they are the fea-tured instrumentalist. While they are playing a lead, every other musician is "laying back," so as not to distract attention from the lead harp. This is some-times called **"taking a solo."** So a **"solo"** means the same as a **"lead."**

Occasionally, a *really* great harp player, like Little Walter or Magic Dick, will get to play an entire song as a lead harp player. More often, good harpists get one verse of solo per song, plus "fills" (page 10). It's also fun to play lead harp by yourself, although it's usually easier to play with accompaniment.

> Harmonica "leads" can be either **classic leads*** (which you memorize and play back at the appropriate time) or **improvised leads** (which you make up on the spot). Almost all blues and rock harp solos are based on the **incredibly useful** and important **blues scale**** (page 62).
>
> * Like Little Walter's eight verse improvised solo song *Juke*, discussed on pages 57 and 64.
>
> ** The blues scale requires "bent" notes, so I'll have to give you a simplified version, for now!

Melody Harmonica

Melody harmonica involves playing mainly the notes of the melody, also called the **tune**, of a particular song. Only a few of the pieces in this book, like *Good Mornin' Blues* and *Frankie and Johnny,* are played melody style. Melodies are always classic pieces, that is, you are playing a piece that someone else created and wrote down. If you get good enough, you can write your own melodies, and other folk will play *them* as classics!

Rhythm Harmonica

Rhythm harmonica is similar to rhythm guitar. The rhythm harpist (or rhythm guitar) provides a nice, solid, **rhythmic background** so that the other players have something to play lead solos along with.

Rhythm harping requires good wind, good timing, and a good knowledge of blues and rock "chord structures," since the rhythm harpist must play the chords along with the rhythm guitarist.

I'll teach you about chord structures later on. "Chord" just means notes that sound right when played together (by keeping your lips open wider).

Rhythm harp is often performed as a combination of classic playing and improvisation. The notes used are determined by the chord structure of the song (classic style), but the harpist may make up his or her own timing patterns on the spur of the moment (improvisation style).

Fill (or "Lick") Harmonica

Fill, or "lick" harmonica provides **musical punc-tuation** for the singer or other instrumentalists. The harp player carefully inserts a few notes, just where they are needed, perhaps between lines, or even between words of a song. These short note combinations are called **"fills," "licks,"** or **"riffs,"** and are almost always based on the blues scale.

Most lead harmonica players also play fills during the verses when the vocalist is singing, or the other instrumentalists are taking solos. Like lead har-monica, fill style playing can be either classic (memorized) or improvised (made up by the player). There are lots of classic licks and fills, and I'll teach you some, soon!

What's Easy, What's Hard?

That's a tough question, since what you'll find easy or hard depends on who you are. If you have a good sense of rhythm and listen to lots of blues and rock music, you'll probably find the improvisation section (Part Six) easier than some of the classic songs. If you like to read, and you're good at following directions, but don't listen to much blues, you may find that playing classic songs is easier than improvisation.

> What's easy or hard really depends on who *you* are, so **try everything,** and if you get stuck anywhere, go on to something else. Then come back to your "sticking point" later on...

An Important Message...

Don't get discouraged, ever. If you're a total beginner and feel a bit clumsy and boggled, just relax, and keep the harmonica in your mouth as you read. You'll get it! If you're a more experi-enced non-blues or rock player who feels "stuck", just remember that all players get into ruts, and a little instruction is a fine way to climb back out.

> No matter what your playing level, or lack of it — the fact that you even have this book in your hands means that you really want to play, or play better. And **wanting** to do it is half the battle, right there!

PART ONE
Basic Harp Technique

Which Harmonica to Use?

You can use any **standard ten hole** harmonica with this book. Some are more expensive, and some are cheaper. But if yours has ten holes, costs between five and thirty bucks (U.S.), and looks more or less like the drawing here, you're probably in good shape.

If you want to be able to play along with the optional tape cassette, you'll need a ten hole harp in the *key of C.*

This kind of harmonica is known by many names: the "ten hole" style harmonica, the "Blues Harp" style, and the "Marine Band" style (these last two are particular models that have been very popular over the years, although many other models exist). More technical names include the **"diatonic"** model or the **"Major-Tuned"** model.

Any harmonica with a slide button ("chromatic" tuned) or with each hole divided in two ("echo" tuned) won't work with this book — but these tunings are less common, anyway. If you'd like to learn to play this type of harp, please see my *Instant Chromatic Harmonica: The Blues/Jazz Improvisation Method*, described on page 63.

How to Hold your Harmonica

Almost any way of holding the harmonica that feels comfortable to you is okay to use. But I suggest using what is technically known as the **"sandwich grip."** This is the way to go if you want to be able to use the important tone effect known as the **"hand wah wah"** (page 37).

Practice holding the harmonica in your left hand, numbers on top, with the lowest note (the #1 hole) to the left. The fingers of your left hand should be in a line, not spread out or separated. **Lefties: Do not reverse!**

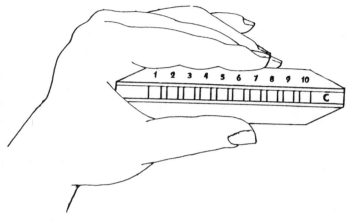

Notes and Chords

Playing any one hole at a time, either inhaling or exhaling, produces what is called a **note**. This is what the single note mouth position looks like — Similar to whistling.

Getting single notes can take a while, so don't worry about it, yet. Playing three (or more) holes at a time will produce a **chord**.

How to Play Chords

Your mouth will just naturally cover about three holes, if you stick your lips over the harp, with your teeth about a quarter-inch apart, and almost but not quite touching the front where the holes are.

Push the harmonica **firmly in between** your lips: Your upper lip should be **well over the top plate** of the harmonica, and your lower lip **well under the bottom plate.** Your upper and lower teeth should be about 1/4 inch apart, and almost touching the holes.

That's why playing harp is sometimes called "eating the tin sandwich". You *shouldn't* feel as though your lips are reaching out to barely kiss a harmonica that's just out of range!

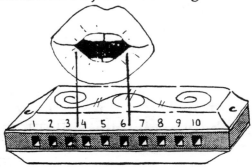

Hold the harmonica any way you like, and play some chords, with your mouth open comfortably wide. You can either breathe in, or breathe out — try it both ways to get two different chords from the same holes.

Play two low chords, by breathing in and then out on the #1, #2, and #3 holes. Now play two high ones, by breathing in and out on the #8, #9, and #10 holes. And now two middle range chords, by breathing in and out on the #4, #5, and #6 holes.

Close Your Nose

Try to breathe through your mouth only when playing — it's a good habit to develop. If you're not sure how to do that, think about blowing out the candles on a birthday cake, or drinking a thickshake through a straw — if your nose weren't temporarily closed off from your mouth, you couldn't do either one very well.   Or picture yourself getting a checkup: Cold stethoscope on your back, and "Breathe through your mouth, please."

Practice trying **not to let any air escape through your nose** while you breathe in and out through the holes of your harmonica. Cover holes #4, #5, and #6, and breathe through the harmonica only for a minute. Pretend it's a snorkel, and you're underwater, and *have* to breathe through it!

HarpTab™

I call my simple harmonica notation system HarpTab™. It tells you which holes to breathe in or breathe out on, and how long to do it for. And as soon as you learn it, you'll be able to play lots of great stuff!

- **The numbers from 1 to 10 tell you which hole to aim your mouth at.**

- **If number is OUTLINED, breathe OUT.**

- **If a number is FILLED IN, breathe IN.**

Here's an example of HarpTab™, but don't even think of trying it yet, unless you feel ready to. You would be breathing out on the first three notes, breathing in on the fourth, then out again on the last four notes.

Fran-	kie	and	John-	ny	were	swe et-hearts
4	5	6	**6**	6	5	4 4

Of course, you probably can't get single notes yet, so let me teach you about chord notation. *Then* you can play something! **(Is reading in English a problem? See below. If not, read on!)**

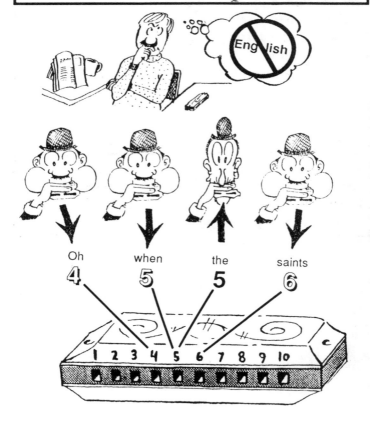

Oh	when	the	saints
4	5	**5**	6

Chord Notation

I show chords, which are notes played together at the same time, by underlining them. Here are two examples: an out chord on holes #4, #5, and #6, then, below, an in chord on holes #1, #2, and #3. In the text, I'll write these chords as 123 in and 456 out, and 8910 out.

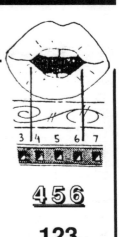

4̲5̲6̲

1̲2̲3̲

Now You Try It!

• Remember, an ⊙u⊡lined number means breathe **out** on that number hole. A number that is **filled in** means breathe **in** on that number hole.

• If you can't play single notes yet, just *aim* your mouth more or less at the hole you want to play, and don't worry. The harmonica is tuned so that it will still sound fine, in most cases, even if you're letting in the holes on either side of the one you really want!

Now aim your mouth at the #4 hole, breathe out, and try playing the first few notes of *Frankie and Johnny.* Just watch the outs and the in note, move your mouth a bit in the right direction when the note numbers change, and don't worry about getting single notes, yet, or about the rhythm.

Fran-	kie	and	John-	ny	were	swe et-hearts
4	5	6	**6**	6	5	4 4

If you aimed at the hole numbers written above, but your mouth was open normally wide, you'd actually be playing these chords below — and they'd sound great:

Fran-	kie	and	John-	ny
3̲4̲5̲	4̲5̲6̲	5̲6̲7̲	**5̲6̲7̲**	5̲6̲7̲

were	sweet-	hearts
4̲5̲6̲	3̲4̲5̲	3̲4̲5̲

Why Chords Work so Well

The notes on the harmonica are arranged so that notes which **"fit together"** well are usually next to each other. That's why we can play *Frankie and Johnny* with either single notes, or with chords based on the correct single note. Playing a chord based on a particular single note just means covering the hole on each side of the desired hole with your mouth. So instead of playing only the note 4 out, you play 345 out, and it sounds fine — rich and full and right!

More Basics

Good Tone, and the #2 In

The key to getting a good tone out of the harmonica is **relaxation.** Try to keep your throat and tongue relaxed, and let your breath come from way down in your belly. If you inhale correctly like this, you will see your stomach fill with air *before* your chest moves.

> If you have trouble getting a good tone out of the #2 in note or chord, you've got lots of company: **The #2 in note on a C harp is tricky!** Lots of beginners would bet that they have a "bad" harp because of this note — but 99% of them would lose! Read this whole section if you're having trouble.

Try ignoring what I said before (about keeping the nose shut), and keep your **nose open** *while* **very gently** inhaling and exhaling on the #2 hole or the 123 in chord. Concentrate on relaxing the back of your throat and your tongue, and you'll find your #2 tone will improve gradually, especially if you play softly. Don't worry about it much, for now — just croak along. It will come!

Where the Heck is Hole # 4?

At first, it's hard to figure out where *any* particular hole is. And even if you don't plan to play a single note, you still need to know where to aim your mouth to get the right chord.

There are three good ways to do it. At first, the easiest way is to bring the harp closer and closer to your mouth, while looking at the numbers on top.

Eventually they'll be too close to see, but by that time you can just pop it into your mouth, and you'll probably be close!

The second way is to point the tip of your tongue, and count your way up (from hole #1) to find the one you need. When you do, just pull your tongue back into your mouth, with the harmonica attached — You'll be right on the hole that you want!

The third way is to put the tip of your finger right on the number of the hole you want on the top cover plate. Then touch that finger to the middle of your upper lip, and you'll be in the right place.

Eventually, you'll be able to know what hole you're on by how the inhale and exhale notes sound, but that takes lots of practice. So for now, look at numbers, count the holes with your tongue-tip, or use your finger.

The Distance Between Holes

Eventually you'll need to learn the distance between holes. It's pretty easy if you're just going from one hole to a neighboring one, like from #4 to #5, or #5 to #6. The actual distance is about 5/16 of an inch, or 8mm (for all the good knowing that does you).

So just move your harp a bit to the right if you want to play the next lower hole, and a bit to the left if you want the next higher hole. In more complicated songs, you'll sometimes need to jump from one hole to another that's two or three holes away. So move farther! **Practice makes perfect!**

The 2 In to 4 Out Jump

Now try the jump from the 123 in chord to the 345 out chord — it's used in lots of blues and rock music. Take your time and go back and forth between them, until you can *feel* the distance!

123   **345**   **123**   **345**

If you didn't have much trouble finding the chords for the first line of *Frankie and Johnny,* or the 123 in to 345 out exercise above, don't bother reading the two sections above this. If you had trouble, well, read 'em, right now — they'll help some.

Telling Time

Keeping the Beat

If you've ever tapped your foot while listening to a piece of music, you know that the **beat** is the steady pulse that underlies a piece of music. Steady beats are all over: In your feet when you walk, in your heart as it pounds, in the windshield wipers of your car.

Practice saying "One Two Three Four" as you tap your foot in a steady beat. If this seems hard to do, you may be "rhythmically insecure". If that's the case, you may want to read about my *Instant Rhythm Kit*, on page 63. Being able to keep a steady beat is really important for us blues and rock harp players, and improving our sense of rhythm is a lifelong job!

HarpTab™ Time

In HarpTab™, I use a **dot** placed above a note to show you where to tap your foot, that is, **where the beat should fall**.

• A dot above a note tells you to begin that note exactly as your foot tap hits the floor.

Try saying "One Two Three Four" again, with a steady beat, while you look at this notation. Catch a quick breathe after each "Four". Don't forget to tap your foot, and begin to say each word *exactly* as your foot hits the floor!

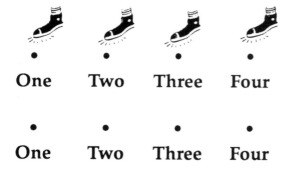

| One | Two | Three | Four |

| One | Two | Three | Four |

Hold the Boxes

Now that you're at the playing part of the book, you don't really need to skim boxes any more. So read the entire next section, and play that train!

> Then, when you run out of steam, take a break, go back to page 6, and start reading the unboxed stuff you skimmed over, before. Or keep on playing some more, if your lips are holding up!
>
> I may still throw in some boxes, to mark really important stuff. But until you see them, start reading every section from here on, and playing each song, lick, fill, and exercise!

The Gravy Train

There is a law — state, federal, and planetary — that says that all harmonica players must be able to sound like a train. This is how you do it — so easy and satisfying that I call it **"The Gravy Train"**. Place your lips so they cover the #1, #2, and #3 holes, then breathe in twice, sharply, and out twice. Almost (but not quite) like two gasps, then two coughs. Can you hear the clacking of those wheels?

Try to keep a **steady beat,** as indicated by the dots above each chord, and also try to keep your **nose shut.** Remember, Outlined means breathe out, **filled in** means breathe in.

·	·	·	·
123	**123**	1̲2̲3̲	1̲2̲3̲

·	·	·	·
123	**123**	1̲2̲3̲	1̲2̲3̲

If your lungs get too **full,** play the in notes softly and the out notes harder for a while. If your lungs feel **empty,** play the in notes more energetically — and you'll get plenty full pretty quickly!

By the way: If your 123 Out chord sounds..."funny," or **"funky"** or **"choked"** — It's probably not a problem with your harmonica. The 2 in can be touchy, for some folk. Review page 16, before you need that note or the 123 in chord again.

About Wooziness

Feel light-headed after that train? Your body is just getting used to processing more air than it's used to. It's natural, at first, but it will pass with a few days or weeks of practice. Until it does, don't play while standing at the edge of a cliff, although I've never heard of anyone actually passing out from it!

More HarpTab™ Time

• A dot without a note under it represents a **beat of silence.** Tap your foot, but *don't* play. Keeping the beat steady during silences is just as important as keeping the beat while you play the notes!

• If a note must be held for **more than one beat**, there will be **more than one dot** above it.

Here is one way of using dots to indicate the beat of *Frankie and Johnny*. The rest of this great melody is on page 26. I'll show you some other ways to notate the beat, later. Notice the four silent beats at the end — use them to catch your breath, before playing the line again!

Remember, don't worry about single notes, yet. Just aim your mouth at what you hope is the right hole to start on (#4 out), watch the **ins** and the **outs**, then move your mouth to where you hope the next hole should be. Play three note chords (wide mouth) if you like, and more than likely, you'll be right enough to sound fine!

From now on, I'll just write down the correct single notes, to save space. If you want to keep playing the notes as chords, be my guest. If a song or lick *requires* single notes, I'll let you know.

•	•	• •	•	•	• •	• •	• •	• • • •
Fran-	kie	and	John-	ny	were	sweet-	hearts	
4	5	6	6	6	5	4	4	

Here are the first notes of a few other songs that you can try to figure out by yourself, if you like.

•	•	•	• • •	• •	•	•	•	• • •	• •
Oh	when	the	saints		go	mar-	chin'	in	
4	5	5	6		4	5	5	6	

•	•	•	•	• • •	• • •	• •
On	top	of	old	Smo-	key	
4	4	5	6	7	6	

PART TWO
What To Do Now

Now that you know how to read HarpTab™, I'll give you a variety of great things to play! Here are some easy but neat-sounding blues licks, rock riffs, and fills, a whistle for your train, and some bluesy folk songs. You can do them in the order written, or pick out the ones that seem most interesting to you, and try those first.

An Easy Blues Lick

Here is a lovely, easy, eight beat blues lick. Make the changes from inhale to exhale quickly and forcefully, and be sure to observe the three silent beats. Do it twice or more, as written. This one will be much more fun with some accompaniment.

· · ·   ·   ·   · · ·

456   **4̲5̲6̲**   **456**

· · ·   ·   ·   · · ·

456   **4̲5̲6̲**   **456**

The Train Whistle

Begin by playing two holes, 45 in, at once. You can do this just by crimping in the corners of your mouth a bit, and puckering *slightly*. Your mouth is a tiny bit less wide than it is for a regular three hole chord, almost as though you were getting ready for a kiss. Take two sharp in breaths, then be silent for two beats. If you begin to practice it in the following timing, it will provide a good whistle for your train!

· · · · · · · ·

4̲5̲ 4̲5̲   **4̲5̲ 4̲5̲**

Practice moving your lips from the 123 out chord to the 45 in chord. Now put your train and your whistle together!

Begin with wheel clacks, and do them for as long as you like. Then throw in your new eight beat whistle pattern once, and return to wheel clacking. The return is easy, since you have two entire beats of silence during which to exhale some air, and get back to the 123 in chord.

The Train with Whistle

123   **123**   123   123

123   **123**   123   123

(play wheels as long as you like, then go to whistle)

45   **45**   **45**   **45**

(return to wheel sounds)

123   **123**   123   123

123   **123**   123   123

An Easy Rock Riff

This eight beat rock riff is somewhat similar to the one used in songs such as **John Mayall's** 1970 blues/rock hit *Room To Move* or the rock classic *Tequila*. I'll present it below as though it were 16 beats long, and in its more standard eight beat form on page 48. Later on, we'll turn it into a great blues/rock lead solo! Make the breath changes, from in to out, and from out to in, fast and forceful.

123   **123**   123

123   **123**   123

123   **123**   123   **123**

(repeat many times)

A Great Blues or Rock Lick

Here's a rhythmically simplified version of one of the world's most popular licks. In its "true" form (page 49), it is really only four beats long, with two silent beats. If you sing during the silent part, the lick becomes a fill! **Muddy Waters** uses a fill similar to this in his beloved *I'm A Man* and *Mannish Boy* songs, as do many blues and rock artists in a variety of songs. You can even hear it used in TV commercials!

Review your jumping from the 123 in chord to the 345 out chord, then try it. I'll write this out, for now, with a tripled beat. So here the fill is twelve beats long — five beats of fill, followed by seven beats of silence — and don't repeat it until you've counted all seven!

123 345 234 123

123 345 234 123

Using it as a Fill

Add a few rhyming vocal lines, and this lick becomes a fill! Make up some rhymes of your own, and go to it!

123 345 234 123

When you play this lick

123 345 234 123

It will real- ly sound slick

123 345 234 123

(continued on next page)

•   •   •   •   •   •   •

If   you just tap your feet

•   ••   •   •

123 **345** **234** **123**

•   •   •   •   •   •   •

It will help keep the beat

•   ••   •   •

123 **345** **234** **123**

Now make up some words of your own, and accompany your own vocals with this riff!

Playing Melodies

These songs will help you get used to using HarpTab™, and also help you learn to move from note to note (or from chord to chord). Remember: I'll write each song down using single notes, but feel free to use the chord based on each note, by keeping your mouth three holes wide, and aiming the middle of your mouth at the note I've written.

The next two sections cover some of the questions that I am most often asked about playing songs.

When Do I Breathe?

Most of the licks, fill, and the train that you've tried so far have had more or less equal amounts of in and out notes, as well as enough beats of silence to use for catching your breath. But some songs have lots of in notes or out notes in a row, so you may need to think, in advance, about how to have just the right amount of air to play the song. I'll discuss the breathing needs of the next three songs when you get to them.

At first, you may need to think about when to breathe during a song. Soon, it will be so natural, you won't even notice catching a breath, any more than you do when you're talking!

"Staccato" or "Legato?"

When you play songs, there are two ways to go from note to note. The term **"staccato"** means to play each note separately and clearly, and us harmonica players usually do this by starting each note with a little separate puff of air. The term **"legato"** means to flow very smoothly from note to note. This requires moving the harmonica in your mouth while gently supplying either an out or in breath, starting each note softly, with no "puff" of air.

Try playing the first two lines of *Frankie and Johnny* in both different ways. Staccato (separate puffs) playing sounds choppier, and legato (flowing) playing sounds sweeter. Both are useful, in places.

What you do not want to do is to take the harmonica away from your mouth in between notes. **Keep your lips wet, and gently slide** the harp from note to note, even if you need to move a long distance.

> You can start each note with a separate puff of air ("staccato" style), or just "flow" from note to note ("legato" style). But whatever you do, **keep your lips moist,** and **slide** from place to place — *Don't move the harp away from your mouth in between notes!*

Playing *Frankie and Johnny*

In the following version of *Frankie and Johnny,* there are more in notes than out notes. So you'd better start each line of the song with your lungs pretty full. By the time you get to an in note, you will have already released enough air to play it.

Fortunately, there are beats of silence scattered throughout the song, so use them to fill your lungs. But be ready for the long in note at the end of the fifth line. Do not fill up too much during the silence at the end of the fourth line — just enough to play the 5 out, 5 in, and 6 out before the long 4 in. And you'll probably need to exhale, and then inhale, during the six beats of silence at the end of the fifth line, or you won't have enough air for the sixth line!

By the way: If you know this classic blues melody well, you may want to ignore the timing dots, and play it to the beat of your different drummer!

Frankie and Johnny

•	•	••	•	•	••	•••	•••	• • • •
Fran-	kie	and	John-	nie	were	sweet-	hearts	
4	5	6	6	6	5	4	4	

C

•	•	••	•	•	••	••••	• • • •
Won-	drous	but	how	they	could	love	
4	5	6	6	6	6	7	

•	••	•	•	••	•	••	°	• • •
They	were	in	true	love	to-	geth-	er	
7	7	6	7	7	6	7	7	

F

•	°	••	••	••	••	••	••
Like	the	stars	that	shine	a-	bove	
6	6	7	7	7	6	6	

C

•	•	••	••••	•••• ••
He	was	her	man	
5	5	6	4	

G

•	•	••	••	•	°
but	he	done	her	wrong	
6	5	6	5	4	

C

•	•	••	••	••••	• • • •
But	he	done	her	wrong	
6	6	6	6	7	

About *Good Mornin' Blues*

Good Mornin' Blues is made up mostly of in notes.
So you'll need start each line with your lungs
pretty empty, and exhale during the silences. But
you'll need to begin the fifth line pretty full, because that line's mostly out notes. Please notice the
three fills, at the end of lines two, four, and six.
This is a good example of a song that combines
melody and fill harmonica.

Good Mornin' Blues

Good	mor-	nin'	Blu-	ues
4	6	⑥	5	4
A7	D7			

Blues	how	do	you	do			
6	⑥	5	4	4		4	4
G7				D7			

Good	mor-	nin'	Blu-	ues
4	6	⑥	5	4
	G7			

Blues	how	do	you	do			
6	⑥	5	4	4		4	4
				D7			

I'm	doin'	all	right	good	mor-	nin'
5	⑤	⑤	⑤	⑤	5	⑤
	A7				G7	

	how	are	you			
	4	4	4		5	4
			D7			A7

The preceding songs were taken from *The Pocket Harmonica Songbook.* If you were able to play these two, you'll be able to play more than twenty of the other songs in that book just as easily! And you'll have twenty that are somewhat more chal-lenging, to work on!

Single Notes?

So far, you haven't needed to play any single notes. If you feel ready to start working on them, turn to page 49, and practice. But you don't require them yet, and really won't until you get to the book *after* this one.

PART THREE
Rhythm Harp and More

In this part of the book, I'll teach you to play some **rhythm harp.** Because even if you never end up needing to hold down the rhythm duties in a blues or rock band, learning to play the following **chord structures** (which is what a rhythm harpist, or rhythm guitarist, does) will help you to improvise later on. Besides, it's easy, fun to do, and sounds good!

> If you're *really desperate* to play more right now, you can go right to the rock and blues chord structures below, and play 'em without reading about 'em. But if you do that, come back and read these sections eventually, because it's good to know what chord structures are, and why they're important.

Songs and Verses

Although the original definition of the word "verse" was "a short division of a chapter in the bible," the word verse now refers to the most basic unit of a song. For example, each of the songs above are one verse long. Most songs consist of from three to ten or so verses. Each verse may have slightly different words, but all the verses are basically quite similar, because they all share the same **chord structure.**

About Chord Structures

As I said before, **chords** are three or more notes that sound good together. A **chord structure** is a set of chords that occur in a **specific order,** with each chord occurring for a **certain number of beats.**

In the version of *Frankie and Johnny* that you played, for instance, the chord structure of each verse takes the form of the chart on page 29. Look back to page 26 and count the beats yourself, if you don't believe me! If you learned ten more verses of this song, each with different words, they would still share exactly the same chord structure. We can describe this song as having a "CFCGC" chord structure. But there is another way, also, to describe this chord structure, using **roman numeral names,** like **I, IV,** and **V.**

Roman Numeral Names

Musicians sometimes refer to chords by **roman numeral names** (I, IV, and V, pronounced "one chord," "four chord," and "five chord") instead of **letter names** (like G, C, and D). So I've included them in this chart — we'll use them, later. The I, IV, and V have **nothing to do** with the **holes # 1, #4,** or **#5** on your harmonica — **Nothing at all!**

Frankie and Johnny Chord Structure

Chord Letter Name	How Many Beats	Roman Numeral Name
C	32	I
F	24	IV
C	8	I
G	16	V
C	16	I

Instrumental Chord Structures

Unlike *Frankie and Johnny,* some chord structures do not have specific lyrics. Instead, they are used to provide a **structure** or **framework** so that the different instruments can play lead solos along with them. I'll teach you to do this in Part Six, when we get around to improvisation. Right now, we are just going to be rhythm harpists, and play the chord structures themselves. But it's good to know what we're *going* to do with them when we can play a bit better.

You might like to think about a chord structure as a **skeleton.** Every one of us has 206 bones — The same 206 bones. But the way those bones are *fleshed out* with muscle, fat, skin and hair can make quite a difference, as looking at Marilyn Monroe and Arnold Schwartzenneger will show you.

Likewise, we can take the skeleton of a chord structure, (as played, or "carried," by a rhythm guitarist or pianist) and flesh it out in *lots of different ways* by playing harp solos along with it: a bluesy solo, a rock solo, or a jazzy solo. It just depends on what notes we choose to play along with the chord structure.

As I said: For now, we're just going to play the chord structure part itself, not try to improvise along with it. And when we're just playing the chord structure by itself (and by ourselves), there's not too much room for variation. All we need to do is to learn some chord structures, starting with some nice, easy ones.

The Simplest Chord Structure

The absolutely simplest chord structure possible is a chord structure made up of only one chord. This kind of chord structure is often called a **"boogie"** (not to be confused with a **"Boogie - woogie,"** which is a type of three chord blues and rock structure).

Although a boogie can be lots of fun to *improvise along with* (we'll do that later), just playing the actual one chord structure is kind of boring, since you would just play the same note or chord over and over and over. Especially now, when you're still limited to playing just one note per beat (we'll fix that, soon). So let's go on to the next simplest chord structure, made up of two chords.

A Two Chord Rock Structure

Many rock chord structures use only two chords, like this one, which uses four beats of Dm (pronounced "D minor") chord (roman numeral name IIm, pronounced "two minor") followed by four beats of C (roman numeral name I). This chord structure sounds best when you leave three of the C chord beats silent. The rockin' song *"Wait,"* by the **J. Geils Band,** has a similar chord structure.

Two Chord Rock Structure

Chord Letter Name	How Many Beats	Roman Numeral Name
Dm	4	IIm
C	4	I

Try to narrow your mouth a bit and get two holes at once, rather than three, and play it twice. Incidentally, this same rock chord structure can also be used as *part* of a blues chord structure.

Your Two Chord Rock Structure

•	•	•	•	•	• • •
45	**45**	**45**	**45**	4̲ 5̲	
Dm				C	

•	•	•	•	•	• • •
45	**45**	**45**	**45**	4̲ 5̲	
Dm				C	

An Easy Single Note to Get

Eventually, you will need to work on getting single notes, that is, playing just one hole at a time. But for now, here's a shortcut for getting a clear, single note out of the #1 hole.

Just put your lips over the #1 hole, or as close to that one hole as you can. Keep them there. Then swivel the high note end of the harmonica *away from your face*. This will push the #1 hole right into your lips, and you'll be able to get a clear, single 1 in note and 1 out note without the 2 in sneaking in.

This swivel technique lets you go from a 123 in chord to a 1 in note very quickly. Which is good, because you'll be needing those 1 notes on your blues turn-arounds and on your '50's Rock and Roll piece!

The Twelve Bar Blues

One special type of chord structure is probably the most popular and widely used chord structure ever — **The Twelve Bar Blues.** It's used not only in blues music, but in rock, pop, and jazz also.

A **bar,** also called a **measure,** is just a term used by musicians to mean **four beats.** (Sometimes a bar could mean three beats, but that's pretty rare in rock or blues music.) **"Twelve bars" is just another way to say "48 beats."**

So a **twelve bar blues** is nothing more than a chord structure that has **48 beats** per verse. And like all chord structures, it uses a particular set of chords (GCGDCG here) that occur in a specific order, with each chord occurring for a certain number of beats.

Start getting used to the **roman numeral names** (I, IV, and V), included in this chart. They'll come in handy, later.

The Twelve Bar Blues **In the Key of G**

Chord Letter Name	How Many Beats	How Many Bars	Roman Numeral Name
G	16	4	I
C	8	2	IV
G	8	2	I
D	4	1	V
C	4	1	IV
G	8*	2*	I*
Totals:	48	12	*includes turnaround

The twelve bar blues chord structure is also known as the **"blues progression"** (since the chords progress from one to the other in each verse), the **"standard blues,"** or the **"blues changes"** (since the chords change from one to the other during the verse). If you'd like to know more about this and other chord structures, you might enjoy checking out my book *Music Theory Made Easy*, on page 63.

Turnarounds

Many chord structures end each verse with what is called a **"turnaround"**. A turnaround is just a **small chunk of V chord** (from two to four beats worth) at the end of a verse that lets you know that one verse is ending, and another is about to begin. Using a turnaround is generally considered classier than shouting "Hey — This verse is over!"

Practice this easy four beat turnaround. Tap your foot, don't forget to include the beat of silence, and remember to keep the 1 in as single as you can by swiveling the high end away. Practice doing a couple in a row if you like, but remember that you'll only use it once per verse in "real life."

123   **1**   **1**

The Easiest Blues Structure

Here's the simplest way to play a twelve bar blues in **cross**, or **second**, **position** (see page 63 for more position info). Of course, you're welcome to use the 123 in chord and 345 out chord in place of the single notes 2 in and 4 out that I've written down.

You've already practiced the two hardest parts: the 123 in to 345 out jump, and the turnaround at the end of the verse. Plus, the two chord rock structure, which you already know, is used as part of it (the fifth line), so you're ready to roll!

Use the beats of silence at the end of each bar of 123 in chord to empty out some air if you feel too full, which you will.

Play this twelve bar verse, then go straight from the final beat of silence at the end to the first 2 in at the beginning and play it again. Get used to playing three or four verses without stopping, and the chord changes of the twelve bar blues will work their way deep into your mind and soul...

A Basic Twelve Bar Blues

```
•   •   •     •   •   •     •
2   2   2     2   2   2
G

•   •   •     •   •   •     •
2   2   2     2   2   2
G

•   •   •     •   •   •     •
4   4   4     4   4   4
C

•   •   •   •   •   •   •   •
2   2   2     2   2   2
G

•     •     •     •     •    •••
45    45    45    45    4 5
D                         C

•   •   •     •   •   •     •
2   2   2     2   1   1
G             D
```

Fleshing Out the Blues

We'll move beyond strict rhythm harp for a few moments, and play a twelve bar blues that is fleshed out a bit by using more than one note or chord for each bar of the structure.

This blues verse is built on a simple **theme.** A theme, or **motif,** is a musical idea that is carried throughout a verse. In this case, the basic theme consists of playing three notes, with each one higher than the last. The actual notes that we use vary depending on which chord of the chord structure is happening, but the basic theme remains, well, basically the same.

Use a sharp, staccato attack on each note (or chord, since you may still not be able to get clear single notes yet). As you know, use a 123 in chord in place of each of my 2 in single notes, a 234 in for my 3 in notes, a 345 in for my 4 ins, a 345 out for my 4 outs, and so on. You might want to practice the new turnaround (the last four beats) for a minute before playing the whole thing.

A Filled Out Twelve Bar

```
 •    •    •    °    •    •    •    •
 2    3    4         2    3    4
 G

 •    •    •    •    •    •    •    •
 2    3    4         2    3    4

 •    •    •    •    •    •    •    •
 4    5    6         4    5    6
 C

 •    •    •    •    •    •    •    •
 2    3    4         2    3    4
 G

 •    •    •    •    •    •    •    •
 4    5    6         4    5    6
 D              C

 •    •    •    •    •    •    •    •
 2    3    4         2    2    1
 G                        D
```

The Basic Boogie Woogie

The **Boogie Woogie** is a special type of **Twelve Bar Blues.** It's based on a early 20th century New Orleans style of piano playing. Try this simple but classic version with a staccato attack on each note. It's a bit more fleshed out than the last twelve bar, since it uses a greater variety of notes.

This piece blurs the distinction between rhythm harp and lead harp. You can play it over and over, as rhythm harmonica, and let another instrumentalist play a solo "on top" of it. Or it could make a fine harp solo — either played by itself, or played along with another instrument that's carrying the rhythm (though an experienced harpist would probably play a fancier version of it for a lead solo).

Your Basic Boogie Woogie

2 3 4 5̄ 5 5̄ 4 3
G

2 3 4 5̄ 5 5̄ 4 3

4̸ 5̄ 6̄ 6 7 6 6̄ 5̄
C

2 3 4 5̄ 5 5̄ 4 3
G

4 5 6 5 4̸ 5̄ 6̄ 5̄
D   C

2 3 4 5̄ 5 5̄ 4 3
G

The 50's Rock Chord Structure

From *Duke of Earl* to *Earth Angel,* the four chords of this rock structure shook the world in the 1950's! Here is the simplest version. Remember to keep the 1 outs (four separate notes) and 1 in (one note held for three beats) as single as you can. Want to try getting single on the 2 out notes, too (page 49)?

2 2 2 2   2̄ 2̄ 2̄ 2̄
G   Em

1̄ 1 1 1   1
C   D

Building on the Rock

Here's a fleshed out verse of the rock chord structure. It would make a simple but effective harp solo played soulfully in the midst of a 50's rock song.

```
 •    •    •    •        •    •    •    •
 2    3    4    5        2    3    3    4
 G                       Em

 •    •    •    •     • • •              •
 1    2    3    2        1
 C                       D
```

A Souped Up 50's Model

I can't resist giving you a fancier version of the rock chord structure right now. But to do that, we'll have to pretend that it has twice as many beats as it really does. Once you've tried it a few times, tap your foot twice as fast as you did for the simpler version, and play this one at the same speed.

```
 ••   ••   ••   •    •
 2    2    2    2    3
 G

 ••   ••   ••   •    •
 2    2    2    2    3
 Em

 ••   ••   ••   •    •
 1    1    1    1    2
 C

 • • • •        •    •    •    •
 1              1    2    1
 D
```

Chaining Verses

"Chain" some of the blues or rock verses that you've just learned together, to form a short song made up of a few verses. Just play one right after the other, without a break — It works!

The Hand Wah Wah

I would prefer to keep tone effects out of this book, but I know that many of you can hardly wait to work on your **hand wah wah.** So hold your harmonica in the left hand sandwich grip (page 12). Keep the fingers of your left hand together.

• Put the part of your right palm that's just above the wrist against your left thumb, as pictured.

• Keep your right palm and left thumb pressed together (in fact, pretend that they are hinged together).

• Swivel your right hand back and forth from the wrist. Try to form a "cup" shape with your hands, that you can open and close by moving your right hand only — an inch or two is enough.

This will block and unblock the area behind your harmonica, and the sound should "wah wah" slightly. Do it slowly and deliberately, or as a fast, fluttering, motion.

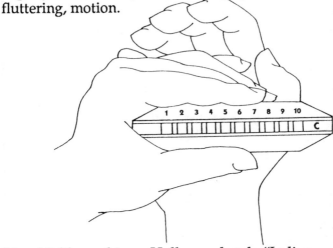

It's a bit like making a Hollywood style "Indian War Whoop" (although I don't believe that actual Native Americans did that at all) motion at the back side of your harmonica.

If the sound doesn't seem to change much, that's because the wah wah sounds better to someone in front of you, than it does to you. We harpists call that **"the wah is always greener on the other side"** syndrome.

Apply the hand wah wah the long 1 in notes of the 50's rock pieces, or anywhere else that a note is held for more than one beat. I'll help you to hone this technique, and use it in different ways, in the next book.

PART FOUR
The Art of Articulation

Now that you can play a variety of chord structures, songs, and licks using just one note or chord
per beat, it's time to learn to use notes that are held
for **less than one beat.** If you don't think you have
"a good sense of rhythm," the optional cassette
that I've recorded to go along with this book may
become somewhat *less* optional. That's because it's
easier to learn rhythm by hearing it than by reading
about it. But, rhythmic or not, give these next
exercises and songs a try, and see how they feel!

Trickier Timing

> Sometimes notes are held for **less than one
> beat.** I indicate this by placing the dot over the
> note on which the beat should fall (when your
> **foot taps** *down*), with **no dot** over the note that
> follows it (when your **foot comes** *up*). So *Yan*
> and *kee* share one beat (one half beat each), as
> do *Doo* and *dle, went* and *to,* and *Lon* and *don.*
>
> Watch the dots and the "down ups" and tap it
> out, as you hum it. Then see if you can play it,
> slowly. Of course, it's always harder to split a
> beat when you have to change from one hole to
> another hole, or from an in breath to an out.

down	up	down	up	down	up	down	up
•		•		•		•	
Yan-	kee	Doo-	dle	went	to	Lon-	don
4	4	**4**	5	4	5	**4**	3

Tap your foot and try these three sets of exercises
on the next page. The first line of each uses one
note per beat, the second line uses two notes per
beat. Tap your foot slower for the second line of
each exercise, and they should sound the same. In
the two notes per beat exercises, the note under the
dot should sound exactly as your **foot hits the
floor,** and the note that is not under the dot should
sound as your **foot is rising up** off the floor.

IMPORTANT: Notice the — symbol at the end of
the second, fourth, and sixth lines, which tells you
to **cut the note to the left of it off sharply.**

.	.	.	.	.	.	.	.
2	**2**	**2**	**2**	**2**	**2**	**2**	
down	up	down	up	down	up	down	up

.		.		.		.	
2	**2**	**2**	**2**	**2**	**2**	**2**	—

.	.	.	.	.	.	.	.
2	**3**	**2**	**3**	**2**	**3**	**2**	
down	up	down	up	down	up	down	up

.		.		.		.	
2	**3**	**2**	**3**	**2**	**3**	**2**	—

.	.	.	.	.	.	.	.
2	**3**	**2**	**3**	**2**	**2**	**2**	
down	up	down	up	down	up	down	up

.		.		.		.	
2	**3**	**2**	**3**	**2**	**2**	**2**	—

Swing Timing & Notation

Blues musicians, seeing this version of *Frankie and Johnny*, would want to **"swing"** the beat. Swinging the beat can only happen when two notes occur during one beat.

.		.	.		.	.	.	.	.
Fran-	kie	and	John-	ny	were	sweet-	hearts		
4	**5**	**6**	**6**	**6**	**5**	**4**	**4**		

Swinging the beat means holding the note that begins right **on** the beat (like the *Fran*, which is under a dot) for a little bit **longer** than the next note which doesn't begin on a beat (like the *kie*, which isn't under a dot). You'd probably want (if you were an experienced blues musician) to play *Fran* a little **louder** than *kie*,, as well as a little longer.

An easy way to hear what swing timing should sound like is to triple the number of timing dots, as I've done below. Tap as fast as you comfortably can, since by tripling the number of dots, each dot should only be played for one third as long as the "real" dots. Notice my loudness indications, too.

loud		loud					
••	•	•••	••	•	•••	•••	••• •••
Fran-	kie	and	John-	ny	were	sweet-	hearts
4	5	6	6	6	5	4	4

Can you go back and make the version on the last page sound just like the triple beat version above? If you can, you're swingin' the beat on *Frankie and Johnny!*

Articulation and Rhythm

It's hard to play lots of clear, sharp notes that don't last for very long. It's especially hard to do it with separate breaths of air. So harp players use a technique called **"articulation."**

Articulation just means breaking up a breath into pieces, by using your tongue to whisper **"dahs" or "tahs" or "kahs"** through the harmonica *while* you play the notes with *one long breath*, instead of using separate breaths of air for each note. With each "tah" (the syllable that I usually use, although you're welcome to try "dah" or "kah") your tongue blocks and then releases your breath, whether it's an in breath or an out breath. This creates a **sharp little puff of air** for each "tah." You should probably practice the examples under this box for a minute.

Here's the first line of *Yankee Doodle.* Try articulating the first two exhaled #4 notes, as I have described here, by whispering some "dahs" right through your 4 out (or 345 out chord). Keep your nose shut tightly!

dah	dah						
•	•	•		•		•	
Yan-	kee	Doo-	dle	went	to	Lon-	don
4	4	**4**	5	4	5	**4**	3

If you want, you can whisper a "dah" on every note, like this. Sometimes you'll want to play each note so that it blends into the next (that is, without any articulation). And sometimes you'll want to emphasize each note sharply, like this, for a more "staccato" or "separate" sound.

dah	dah	dah	dah	dah	dah	dah	dah
•		•		•		•	
Yan-	kee	Doo-	dle	went	to	Lon-	don
4	4	**4**	5	4	5	**4**	3

Articulation on the in breath is a bit less natural than on the out, since we mostly talk on the out breath. *Empty* your lungs, *shut* your nose, close your eyes (for concentration) and set your lips over the 4 in, or the 345 in chord..

Whisper a bunch of tahs through your harp *while* **you inhale.** Don't worry about speed or timing — Just make your tongue create a tah sound while you inhale. It's the exact tongue motion that you use on the exhale, but you're much more used to doing it that way! So practice!

Some Articulation Patterns

Here are two useful articulation patterns, **"taah ta ta"** and **"ta ta taah."** I will notate these for the #4 out and 2 in notes, but use the 345 out and 123 in chords if you need to, and try these same rhythm patterns on a number of different notes and chords.

Notice that the "ta" is a shorter note, only half as long as the "taah." Here, the taah represents one whole beat, and the ta represents half a beat. The timing dots will help you to remember this, so keep an eye on them as you play.

taah	ta	ta	taah	ta	ta
•	•		•	•	
4	4	4	4	4	4

taah	ta	ta	taah	ta	ta
•	•		•	•	
2	**2**	**2**	**2**	**2**	**2**

ta	ta	taah	ta	ta	taah
•		•	•		•
4	4	4	4	4	4

ta	ta	taah	ta	ta	taah
•		•	•		•
2	**2**	**2**	**2**	**2**	**2**

Articulation Training

Go back to page 19 and whisper "chugga" through your train — Swing it a little, even. All aboard!

chug-	ga	chug-	ga
•		•	
123	**123**	**123**	**123**

chug-	ga	chug-	ga
•		•	
123	**123**	**123**	**123**

Two Licks and a Boogie

Starting to get used to these tas and taahs? Try using them, on the next page. The first two lines provide a simple **boogie** (one chord structure) in the style of **Canned Heat's** late harpist, the talented **Blind Owl Wilson**. This boogie may sound better using 123 in chords instead of 2 in notes. We'll also add two eight beat **licks** to our boogie.

Tap your foot! Make sure the notes under the dots happen exactly as your foot hits the floor, with the notes not under dots happening in between taps. Be aware that **some** of the 2 ins, and the 34 in and 45 out chords, are held for a **whole beat**. Keep your lips wet, and don't take them away from the harmonica — **glide and slide** from note to note.

As you can see, the second lick has two notes during the second and sixth beats. But instead of using "tahs," just slide your lips from note to note, without the puff of air that the tahs provide. But make sure you keep the timing correct: Tap your foot, and watch it! Play each part of this — The boogie, and the first and second licks — separately before attempting to play the entire thing straight through, as I describe below.

John Lee Hooker Style Boogie

Play the boogie four times, then play the first lick once, then play the boogie four more times. Then play the second lick once, return to the boogie, and play it a few more times before fading out to nothing . It'll sound like a **John Lee Hooker** and **Canned Heat** boogie from the late 60's. Start out with your lungs pretty empty, or else!

taah   ta   ta   taah   ta   ta

2   **2**   **2**   **2**   **2**   **2**

taah   ta   ta

2   **2**   **2**   **34**   **4 5**

(play above boogie **three** more times)

First Lick

ta   ta   taah   ta   ta   taah

4   **3**   **2**   **4**   **3**   **2**

ta   ta   taah taah

4   **3**   **2**   **2**

(then back to the boogie)

taah   ta   ta   taah   ta   ta

2   **2**   **2**   **2**   **2**   **2**

taah   ta   ta

2   **2**   **2**   **34**   **4 5**

(play above boogie **three** more times)

Second Lick

4   **4**   **3**   **2**   **4**   **4**   **3**   **2**

(then back to the boogie)

taah   ta   ta   taah   ta   ta

2   **2**   **2**   **2**   **2**   **2**

taah   ta   ta

2   **2**   **2**   **34**   **4 5**

(play above boogie a few more times and **fade out**)

"Dirty Dog" Articulations

I sometimes like to use "dirty dog" articulations. They're kind of silly, but they help to give me (and many other harp players, especially beginners) a better sense of swing timing. Say a few, without your harmonica, but do tap your foot and watch the silent beat at the end. **Say the *dir* louder and longer than the *ty*.** I'll start out with three times the real number of beats.

· ·	·	· ·	·	· · ·		· · ·
Dir-	ty	**Dir-**	ty	**Dog**		

Now try swinging your dogs without using the extra dots. Tap your foot down on the dir, say the ty while your foot comes up, and say it just as you did in the last version.

·		·		·		·
Dir-	ty	**Dir-**	ty	**Dog**		

Whisper some dirty dogs on various out notes, then try whispering it on some in notes. Here are a few suggestions (doing it on the 2 in or 123 in will be really useful, so practice that one lots), but use other notes and chords too. Start *empty* on the dirty dog in articulations, and keep that nose closed! Swing 'em!

·		·		·		·
Dir-	ty	**Dir-**	ty	**Dog**		
4]	4]	4]	4]	4]		

·		·		·		·
Dir-	ty	**Dir-**	ty	**Dog**		
4	4	4	4	4		

·		·		·		·
Dir-	ty	**Dir-**	ty	**Dog**		
2	2	2	2	2		

Swing Time Blues

If you've practiced the three dog rhythms just above, use them in a blues structure that swings. It's almost the same as the one you did on page 33, except that most of the notes come two to the beat, instead of one. To save space, instead of writing out each of the first four bars, I've written down one, and told you to repeat it three more times. Work your tongue! Articulate!

Dir-	ty	Dir-	ty	Dog	
•		•		•	ο
2	**2**	**2**	**2**	**2**	

G

(repeat above bar **three** more times)

Dir-	ty	Dir-	ty	Dog	
•		•		•	•
4	**4**	**4**	**4**	**4**	

C

Dir-	ty	Dir-	ty	Dog	
•		•		•	•
4	**4**	**4**	**4**	**4**	

C

Dir-	ty	Dir-	ty	Dog	
•		•		•	•
2	**2**	**2**	**2**	**2**	

G

Dir-	ty	Dir-	ty	Dog	
•		•		•	•
2	**2**	**2**	**2**	**2**	

G

Dir-	ty	Dir-	ty	Dog	
•		•		•	•
45	**45**	**45**	**45**	**45**	

D

Dir-	ty	Dir-	ty	Dog	
•		•		•	•
45	**45**	**45**	**45**	**45**	

C

Dir-	ty	Dir-	ty	Dog	
•		•		•	•
2	**2**	**2**	**2**	**2**	

G

Dog	Dog	Dog	
•	•	•	•
2	**1**	**1**	

D

More Articulations

Sometimes articulations are used to change the sound quality of a note or chord, instead of using them to break a note into pieces.

A Good Whistle Articulation

Let's go back to the train whistle. But this time, use an **"oy"** articulation on each chord — that is, whisper "oy" while you play the chord. How? Just whisper "oy" as you **inhale** on each 45 in chord. Lungs empty, nose closed, and do exactly the reverse of what you do when you say "oy" on an out breath.

Exaggerate the motion of your tongue as you "oy," but keep your lips steady on just the #4 and #5 in. This adds an even more train-like quality to your whistle, and will begin to help you bend, eventually, since the "oy" tongue motion is somewhat similar to certain bending motions. Practice and then go back to the train (page 22) and use your new "oy" whistle.

oy	oy			oy	oy		
°	°	•	•	°	•	•	•
45	**45**			**45**	**45**		

A Dylan Style Fill

Bob Dylan is not a blues harp player, and this fact motivates some blues harpists to minimize his harmonica abilities. However, since he is a master musician whose music has moved an entire generation, I consider him a *virtuoso*, blues harpist or not.

This fill is similar to many that he inserts into his talking blues style songs. Crimp your lips down to get two holes, and inhale an exaggerated "oy" whisper as I've notated it, like the train whistle.

oy	oy	oy			
•	•	•	•	•	• • •
45	**45**	**45**	**4 5**	**34**	

oy	oy	oy			
•	•	•	•	•	• • •
45	**45**	**45**	**4 5**	**34**	

Dwah-ing the Two Chord Rock

Add a "dwah" type articulation to the Two Chord Rock Structure. It's just like and "oy" articulation, except that you're whispering "dwah" on the in breath. Practice saying a few "dwahs" on the out breath, without harmonica. Then start really empty, keep your nose shut, and try this!

dwaah	dwaah	dwaah	dwaah	
•	•	•	•	• · · ·
45	**45**	**45**	**45**	**45**

Now Dwah - Dah It!

If you'd like to try a harder articulation, use the popular "dwah dah" combination on a two chord per beat version of the rock two chord structure.

As you can see, each "dwah dah" breaks each 45 in into two parts, with the two parts one half beat long each. There are also some longer "dwaahs," held for an entire beat.

First say a few "dwah dahs" on the out breath, without the harp, to learn the tongue motion. Then say a few, without harp, on the in breath. Practice a few dwah dahs on the 45 in chord , then play this. It's pretty hard, but practicing will help you learn to bend, later on! Also: Adding a dwah to the 34 in of the **Hooker Boogie** (page 43) will sound great!

dwaah	dwah	dah	dwah	dah
•	•		•	
45	**45**	**45**	**45**	**45**

dwah	dah		
•		•	• •· •
45	**45**	**45**	

Swinging the Oldies

If you are getting the feel of the swing beat (and mastering swing timing is an art form, and can take a lifetime), try applying it to some of the songs you already know. But if this seems difficult, don't be discouraged — Just continue to play the older, non-swing versions, since in the sequel to this book we will work on timing in much greater detail.

For example, the **Basic Boogie Woogie** on page 35 can be played as a swing piece very simply. Just play each note twice instead of once, and make the first note of each pair a bit longer and louder than the second note of each pair. Here's what the first line from page 35 would look like as a **Swing Boogie Woogie.**

•		•		•		•	
2	**2**	**3**	**3**	**4**	**4**	5	5

•		•		•		•	
5	**5**	5	5	**4**	**4**	**3**	**3**

You could also do something very similar with the blues from the *Fleshing Out the Blues* section on page 34. That blues will sound great if you apply the "dirty dirty dog" rhythm pattern to each bar of the twelve bar structure. This is what the first bar (first four beats) would look like — Use your tongue and apply the same rhythm to the **other eleven bars** for a swell twelve bar blues.

dir	ty	dir	ty	dog	
•		•		•	•
2	**2**	**3**	**3**	**4**	

Swinging Riffs and Licks

Now would be a good time to take two licks that you already know, and practice them with their "real" timing.

Here's the **Easy Rock Riff,** written out with only half as many timing dots as it was on page 22, when you first learned it. To save space, I'm also going to write it out as 2 in and 2 out instead of 123 in and 123 out. But this one really sounds better played with chords, than with single notes. Practice the old version, then play:

•		•		•		•	
2	**2**	2		**2**	**2**	2	

•		•		•	•	
2	**2**	2	**2**			

And this is the **Great Blues or Rock Riff,** from page 23, also written out with only half as many timing dots. This makes it hard to read, since it starts in between beats. To *begin* playing a series of this riff, count to three, then start it *before* you would have said "four." I'll write it in single notes, but play it with chords if you like to, or need to. Practice the old version, then play this one. It's played as cross or second position harp, in the key of G.

			up	down	up	down			
•	•	•	•	•	•	•	•	•
"one"	"two"	"three"	**2**	**4**	**3**	**2**		

up	down	up	down					
	•		•	•	•		•	
2	**4**	**3**	**2**		**2**	**4**	**3**	**2**

(repeat many more times)

Single Notes

Now that you've practiced playing three note chords and two note chords, you may want to start working on getting single notes on holes other than the 1. It's tricky at first, but eventually you should try to learn it. Luckily, pretty much everything in this book can be played without mastering single notes.

Pucker your lips, so that the hole formed by your mouth is just a bit bigger than a harmonica hole. It's the same mouth shape that you use when you're whistling, or drinking through a straw.

Mouth Hole Shape

Your upper lip should be slightly curled up towards your nose, like a dog snarling. Try to keep your tongue and throat muscles relaxed, even though your lip muscles may feel tense when first learning to play.

Work on single noting the #1 hole, both in and out — it's the easiest, since there is no #0 to get in the way on the left. Listen closely, and make sure that you don't let any of that #2 note creep in! It may be easier to practice single noting if you don't try to do it loudly, at first. Just relax, crimp those lips, and try it.

Single notes become increasingly important if you get more serious about your playing. So — Beginners — **Don't get hung up here,** but do come back and practice!

By the way — an advanced single noting method known as **tongue blocking** is often used to play polkas and for special effects. In this method, the mouth covers four holes, and the tongue is used to block three, so only one plays. But don't worry about this way of playing, until later on, unless you can already do it.

Six Blow Practice

The note 6 out is one of the most important single notes to get, so it's worth a bit of practice. If necessary, put a finger on the number 6 of the cover plate to locate the right hole.

When you start to be able to get a more or less single 6 out at least once in a while, try "tah-ing" it, like this.

tah	tah	tah		tah	tah	tah	
•	•	•	•	•	•	•	•
⑥	⑥	⑥		⑥	⑥	⑥	

Blues Scale Prep

Now might be a good time to practice some note combinations that will help prepare you for the blues scale, which I'll begin to discuss on page 62. It's a good way to motivate yourself to practice single notes! Since the 6 out, 5 in, and 4 in are blues scale notes, being able to move around amongst them is a great skill for a beginning harpist to cultivate. Try these simple blues and rock licks!

•	•	•	•	•	•	•	•
⑥	5	4		⑥	5	4	

•	•	•	•	•	•	•	•
4	5	⑥		4	5	⑥	

•	•	•	•	•	•	•
4	5	⑥	5	4		

PART FIVE
Famous Licks and Styles

A Word of Respect

The following harmonica players have devoted their lives to giving us the gift of music, so we all owe them a great deal of re-spect. I've been lucky enough to meet, and even play with, some of them. I especially want to acknowledge the depth of my feeling for my friends **Mr. J. C. Burris** (left) and his uncle **Sonny Terry.** Their passing has made our world a grayer place...

Famous Licks, Solos, and Styles

I want to give you a "taste" of the way in which different artists handle our favorite instrument. It's hard to pick out only the work of a few, but I've created my own **arrangements** (customized original versions) in the styles of some famous players.

Certain of these arrangements are **generic,** that is, nearly everyone uses them at some time or another. Others are more clearly in a specific artist's style, even though many players may do something similar, or even the same. Most of them can be played solo (unaccompanied), but they will sound even better with some keyboard or guitar backing.

IT IS CRUCIAL to buy and listen to any albums, tapes, or CD's that you can find which feature these, and other master harp players. If you don't already have a good blues harpist record collection, read about the Blues Masters CD/Tape on page 64.

"Mixing and Matching"

Many of the licks and parts of solos that you're learning are **interchangable.** You can combine them in various ways to create a whole new solo. This will help you to start improvising, in Section Six.

The Accent Mark: '

These licks and solos will sound better if you **"accent"** certain notes — Play them a little bit harder than the rest. I'll use a mark like this ' next to the timing dot over the note I want you to accent. Play it louder!

A Generic Lick or Ending

This eight beat lick can be used as a (slightly repetetive) lead solo during a twelve bar blues or rock structure, simply by playing it six times (six times x eight beats = 48 beats = 12 bars). Or, it makes an excellent **"ending"** (last eight beats of a verse) for almost any twelve bar.

2   2   2   2   2   2̲   1   1

About Intros

An **"intro"** is an **introduction** to a song. Blues and rock intros are usually **sixteen beats long,** and, of course, come just before the first verse of the song. An intro is very much like the last sixteen beats of a twelve bar chord structure, except that it comes before the verse starts. I'll teach you a great intro soon.

James Cotton Style Lick/Ending

I had the pleasure of touring briefly with **James Cotton** (as well as with the late Chicago stylist Paul Butterfield, and country/jazz harpist extraordinaire Norton Buffalo) in a short series of "Harmonica Summits" in late 1982. Although far from the only one to use this lick/ending, it's one that I often associate with Mr. Cotton.

Like the generic lick/ending above, it can be played six times to create a lead solo in a twelve bar, or used as the last eight beats of a solo. Try it both ways, especially with some blues or rock accompaniment. Accent every other beat, as I've indicated.

2   3   4̲   4̲   2   2̲   1   1

A Cotton Style Intro

We can create a great "mix and match" sixteen beat **intro** by combining two bars of the Swing Blues from page 45 with the Cotton style ending. Put this **in front** of any of the twelve bar blues (or a series of them that you've chained together, as I said on page 36) for a dynamite full length blues song!

•		•		•	•
Dir-	ty	**Dir-**	ty	**Dog**	
45	**45**	**45**	**45**	**45**	
D					

•		•		•	•
Dir-	ty	**Dir-**	ty	**Dog**	
45	**45**	**45**	**45**	**45**	
C					

•′	•	•′	•	•′	•	•′	•
2	**3**	**4**	**4**	**2**	**2**	**1**	**1**
G						D	

A New Rock Riff, Then Twelve Bar

With one new rock lick to fit into the "C (or IV) chord" section of the twelve bar, you'll be able to play a hot twelve bar rock verse that's reminiscent of English harp master **John Mayall (or Sonny Boy Williamson II's *One Way Out*)**. First practice **The Easy Rock Riff** on pages 22 and 48 ("G or I part").

Then play the *C Chord version* of the **Easy Rock Riff** with doubled dots below, and when that gets easy, try the "real time" version beneath it.

•	•	••	•	•	••
45	**45**	**34**	**45**	**45**	**34**

•	•	•	•	• • •
45	**45**	**34**	**45**	

•	•	•	•	•
45	**45**	**34**	**45**	**45**	**34**

•	•	••
45	**45**	**34**	**45**

Mr. Mayall (who helped shape the career of Eric Clapton and numerous other top English and American blues artists) likes to use chords more than single notes, with explosive, percussive, in and out breath patterns. So use 123's here, not 2's.

The entire twelve bar rock solo starts out with **two** of the **Easy Rock Riffs,** followed by **one** of the new **C Chord Rock Riffs,** then **one more** of the **Easy Rock Riffs.** Then add the "dwah" version of the **Two Chord Rock Structure** (page 47) or, if you're adventurous, the "dwah dah" version. End your verse with **one last Easy Rock Riff,** and you're done — There's no turnaround!

The Hot Rock Twelve Bar

dwaah	dwaah	dwaah	dwaah			
•	•	•	•	•	•	• • •
45	**45**	**45**	**45**	**45**		
D				C		

•		•		•		•
2	**2**	**2**		**2**	**2**	**2**
G						

•		•	•	•
2	**2**	**2**	**2**	

Sonny Terry Style Rhythm Harp

The late **Sonny Terry,** and his nephew, the late **J. C. Burris,** were two of the world's greatest **country blues** harmonica stylists. Born in the Piedmont region of North Carolina, they played the bouncy, chordy, good time **Piedmont Style Blues.**

This is a rhythm pattern that they often used, with lots of variations. Play it slowly until you get the feel of it, try to keep the 1 in single (swivel, if necessary), and remember to move a bit higher to get the 234 out chord when you need it. Play it repeatedly, and increase your speed.

	ta	ta	ta	ta	
•	•	•	•	•	•
123	**123**	**123**	**123**	**123**	**1**

	ta	ta			
•	•	•		•	•
123	**123**	**123**	**234**	**123**	

Playing a Sonny Terry Style Solo

Once you have the hang of the rhythm pattern, add a few **Piedmont Style Licks** to create a boogie (one chord) type solo in the key of G. You'll definitely need to practice the 45 in to 6 out jump for a while.

If you like, you can **"shake"** the long 45 in. To do this, make your mouth hole as small as possible. Lick your lips, then shake the harmonica slightly from side to side (most players use their right hand to control the movement) so that your mouth hole alternates between the 4 in and the 5 in. It will come, with practice. I notate this with a wavy line beneath the 45 in. Or, if you like, just play a long 45 in without the shake.

	ta	ta	ta	ta	
•	•	•	•	•	•
123	**123**	**123**	**123**	**123**	**1**

	ta	ta		
•	•	•	•	•
123	**123**	**123**	**234**	**123**

	ta	ta	ta	ta	
•	•	•	•	•	•
123	**123**	**123**	**123**	**123**	**1**

	ta	ta		
•	•	•	•	•
123	**123**	**123**	**234**	**123**

• • • • •   •   • •

45   **6**

wwww

•	•	•	•	•	•	• • •
45	**45**	**45**	**34**	**2**	**2**	

(repeat two or three more times)

Sonny Boy #1 Style Lick or Ending

Sonny Boy Williamson #1 (who died tragically in 1948) uses this *early Chicago style* lick often, as does **Sonny Terry.** Try it with tripled beats, then without. Then play it twice without the 1 ins, plus once with the 1 ins, for an SBW #1 style lead, in the key of G.

•′	•	•	•′	•	•
3	**4**	**4**	**4**	**3**	**2**

•′	•	•	•′	•	•	•′••	•′	• •
3	**4**	**3**	**2**			**1**	**1**	**1**

•′			•′		
3	**4**	**4**	**4**	**3**	**2**

•′		•′			•′	•′	
3	**4**	**3**	**2**		**1**	**1**	**1** —

Walter Style Lick, Lead, & Ending

Many believe that **Marion "Little Walter" Jacobs** was the greatest harp player ever. It's certainly true that his arrangements were exquisitely thought out, and his tone (enhanced by throat vibrato effects and a judicious use of microphone and amplifier) was superb. In his great song *Juke*, he takes a well-known "pentatonic scale" and adds rhythm to create a killer lick. Practice this scale:

2 3 4 5̶ 6

Add some rhythm with tripled dots first (top line), then see if you can use the actual number of beats (second line), for a Juke style riff. As the accents indicate, stress the beginning of the first 6 out note.

2 3 4 5̶ 6̶ 6̶

2 3 4 5̶ 6̶ 6̶

When you can play the above four beat version, create a twelve bar solo as follows. Play the above four beat **lick eight times.** Then follow it with these lines, being careful to notice the five places where one beat is split into two notes. The **bottom line** is a very characteristic **Little Walter style verse ending,** and can be "mixed and matched" to end many twelve bar verses. **By the way: Every harp player MUST own (if not play)** *Juke,* so see page 63.

2 3 4 5̶ 6̶ 6̶
G

(repeat above lick seven more times to complete the G - C - G or I - IV - I parts of the twelve bar) (Review page 31 if you need to)

4 5̶ 5 5̶ 4 5̶ 6̶
   D

5 5̶ 4 4̶ 3
C

2 2 3 2 2̶ 2 2̶ 1 1
G   D

PART SIX
Beginning to Improvise

Improvisation, or "jamming," means making up your own music as you go along. I'll cover this extensively in the next book, and just give you some easy instructions that will help you to begin improvising right away at a simple level. By the way: Beginners always find it easier to jamm along with accompaniment, rather than by themselves...

I believe that there are three main ways to improvise. The **"Mix and Match"** method is the simplest and the least creative, and involves taking licks that you've already practiced, and combining them in various ways. The **"Chordal Approach"** allows you to improvise by using any of the **notes of the chords** of the twelve bar blues structure. The **"Blues Scalar Approach"** will be heavily featured in the next book, as it is slightly more complex. It allows you to improvise by using any of the **notes of the blues scale.**

Mixing and Matching

Many of the licks and parts of solos that you've learned are **interchangeable.** You can take parts of one, mix it with parts of another, and create a whole new solo. Please review the Twelve Bar Blues Chord Structure Chart on page 31. We'll now create an entire twelve bar blues solo, based on the last line of the Sonny Terry Style Solo.

Repeat that last line (eight beats) four times, to make up the eight bars (32 beats) of the I - IV - I part of the twelve bar.

Then add any Two Chord Rock Structure (like the one on page 30 or on page 47) to make up the V - IV (also called the D - C) part of the twelve bar.

End with any one of the eight beat ending licks, like the Cotton Style one on page 52, or the Generic one. Adding these up totals 48 beats, or twelve bars, and you've created a **mix and match lead solo!**

A Few New V - IV 's to Use

I've given you a number of licks and endings to use, but not too many of the Two Chord Rock Style pieces to use during the **V - IV** or D - C parts (bars nine and ten) of your mix and match twelve bar

eads. So here are a few new ones that I like, which
ou can use interchangeably, of course:

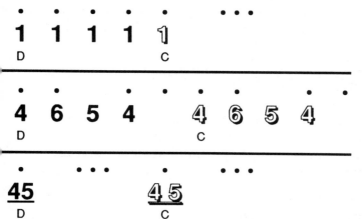

Try a mix and match twelve bar lead using one of
these new V - IV parts. For Example:

Play *any* eight beat **riff** (like the Easy Blues or Rock,
pages 21 or 22) (or the First or Second Boogie Licks,
page 43) four times. These form the eight bars (32
beats) of your I - IV - I. Then use the middle V - IV
above, and finish off with a Cotton Ending (page 52).

You'll need either to *memorize* these pieces from
different pages, or else *write each piece down*, in
order, on a separate page, or else learn to *flip from
page to page quickly*, in between beats! Interestingly,
even good blues harpists often use an "interchangeable" last four bars when they play multiple twelve
bar solos in a row — that is, they **vary** the **first
eight bars** (32 beats) of each verse, but do something **more or less the same** for the **last four bars**
(16 beats) of each verse. So memorize at least one
V - IV part plus ending that you like, and you'll be
ready to plug it in whenever you need it.

Improvising Licks and Solos

Here's a simple way to create four and eight beat
licks of your own. These will be used during the I -
IV - I part (first eight bars, or 32 beats) of a twelve
bar chord structure (then just add a V - IV plus
ending to create an entire solo).

Try doing this **"classic"** style: Experiment with
note combinations that you like, according to my
rules. Write the licks down in a twelve bar structure
when you're satisfied, then play it from your notation.

Or you can do it in true **"improv"** style: Memorize
my Simple Jamming Rules, and at least one V - IV
part plus ending that you like. Then turn the lights
low, try not to think much, and see what happens!

The Simple Jamming Rules

I've invented an **easy, if limited,** way to let you improvise using the **chordal approach** with **three easy to remember rules** (only two of which I'll give you in this book). Each rule works with one of the three chords of the Twelve Bar Blues: One rule for each I chord, one rule for each IV chord, and one rule for each V chord.

For example, all of the **out** notes, from hole 1 to hole 10, provide notes that will fit in during the **IV chord.** How lucky for us! You can begin to use these rules by practicing each rule separately, and using dirty dog rhythms in a new way.

The IV Chord Jamming Rule

This is the easiest rule to start with. All you need to do, is to play **OUT NOTES ONLY,** in some pleasing rhythm pattern (like the four beat dog rhythm), using interesting combinations of various out notes. Here are two examples, but you can use *any out notes,* so don't worry about which notes you're on. Just whisper those dogs, and move around!

•		•		•		•
Dir-	ty	Dir-	ty	Dog		
1	1	2	2	3		

•		•		•		•
Dir-	ty	Dir-	ty	Dog		
5	5	1	1	2		

Eight Beat Dog Rhythms

Now memorize this new eight beat rhythm pattern. Use it with the IV Chord Jamming Rule, to create licks made up only of out notes, in any combinations. Try my examples, then make up some eight beat out jamms of your own. Put 'em together, in a series, to form an out note boogie. It'll sound great with my **Out Boogie Accompaniment!**

•'		•'		•	•	•' • • •
Dir-	ty	Dir-	ty	Ding	Dong	**Dog**

•'		•'		•	•	•' • • •
Dir-	ty	Dir-	ty	Ding	Dong	**Dog**
5	5	4	4	3	2	1

Dir-	ty	Dir-	ty	Ding	Dong	Dog
•´		•´		•	•	•´ • • •
1	1	2	2	3	2	1

The I Chord Jamming Rule

This rule creates licks that fit in during your I chords, but instead of using the out notes only, it uses the **LOW IN NOTES ONLY**, from the **1 in** to the **5 in.** Make up endless variations of your own: Use 1 in to 5 in notes only, keep the rhythm pattern going, and you can't go wrong. Here are some four beat licks I like, but don't just play mine!

Dir-	ty	Dir-	ty	Dog	
•´		•´		•	•
5	5	4	4	3	

Dir-	ty	Dir-	ty	Dog	
•´		•´		•	•
2	2	5	5	2	

Use the new eight beat dog rhythm with the I Chord Jamming Rule. Here are a few examples.

Dir-	ty	Dir-	ty	Ding	Dong	Dog
•´		•´		•	•	•´ • • •
5	5	4	4	3	2	3

Dir-	ty	Dir-	ty	Ding	Dong	Dog
•´		•´		•	•	•´ • • •
2	2	2	2	<u>34</u>	<u>34</u>	2

Since the first I chord part of a twelve bar blues is 16 beats long, practice creating some **sixteen beat combinations.** You can do this by combining two eight beat licks (just play my two examples above, to make up one sixteen beater). Or you can do it by adding one eight beat lick to two four beat licks, like this:

Dir-	ty	Dir-	ty	Dog	
•´		•´		•	•
4	4	3	3	2	

Dir-	ty	Dir-	ty	Dog	
•´		•´		•	•
4	4	3	3	2	

Dir-	ty	Dir-	ty	Ding	Dong	Dog
•´		•´		•	•	•´ • • •
5	5	4	4	3	2	3

A Jamming Rules Twelve Bar

You can create a series of improvised **Jamming Rules Twelve Bar Blues** like this:

Use the **I Chord Rule (1 in** to **5 in** only) for **16 beats** (which could be made up of four four beat licks, two eight beat licks, or two fours plus one eight to make up a sixteen beater).

Use the **IV Chord Rule (any out)** for **8 beats** (which could be two four beat licks, or one eight beater).

Use the **I Chord Rule** again (**1 in** to **5 in** only) for **8 beats** (which could be made up of two four beat licks, or one eight beat lick).

Throw in a **memorized V - IV** combo, then any **eight beat ending,** and you're ready to do another verse, with a different set of improvised I - IV - I first eight bars. Re-read the section on Improvising Licks and Solos, and you're ready to let it rip!

Blues Scale "Teaser" Lick & Ending

I'd love to teach you more about bending, and positions, and the "why" of scales. But we're out of pages. So read a bit about bending and positions in my book descriptions that follow. These are the actual notes of the second position, or cross, blues scale. The little "b" symbols indicate notes that must be bent.

2 3b 4̲ 4b 4 5 6̲

Since you probably can't really bend yet, I'll give you two simple licks that are based on the blues scale, but do not use bends. The first is a great eight beat lick that you can repeat four times to fill in the first eight bars of a twelve bar solo, in mix and match style (page 58). The second is similar, but has a turnaround, so it can be used as an eight beat ending.

6̲ 5 4 4̲ 3 2

6̲ 5 4 4̲ 3 2 2̲ 1 1

Play a great bluesy twelve bar lead by repeating the first lick four times, throwing in any V - IV chunk, then ending with the blues ending lick. It'll sound great, and I'll teach you to do lots more (and make up your own) in the next book!

More Harp Methods

If you liked this book enough to get this far, you might enjoy some of my other products, too. Here they are:

Three Minutes to Blues: The Optional Video

My recent video, *Three Minutes to Blues Harmonica*™, demonstrates many of the licks and solos in this book, and more, using my incredibly effective *Harmonica Hand Signal Method*™. 73 minutes only $12.95! For C harp. Many people consider it THE fastest way to learn harp!

Learning From the Masters: *Juke*, Plus...

I have two great new products for blues lovers. The **Blues Masters Harmonica Classics CD** and **Hint Sheet** is a sampler of 18 classic harmonica songs performed by the original artists, including Little Walter playing *Juke**, Jimmy Reed, James Cotton, Paul Butterfield, Charlie Musselwhite, and more! The "Hint Sheet" tells you which harp to use (with a C and A harp you can play nine songs, add a Bb harp and play 14) and what to do to play along! The CD is $17.95, the cassette (14 song) $9.95, and both come with the invaluable free Hint Sheet!

Another new product is my *Juke* **Tape**. This is a 90 minute tape that describes in detail how to play every note, lick, and solo of the eight verses of this classic blues instrumental, recorded May 12, 1952, originally as Checker single 955 (Licensing: Arc Music Corp., BMI). It's for an A harp, and any level of player can use it (some verses are easy)! $8.95. ***NOTE:** You'll *need* an original recording of *Juke* to use this!

Learning to Improvise — With Instant Blues Harmonica, Volumes I & II

Volume I is our classsic blues only method, used by over 150,000 satisfied customers! Although some of the material is the same as in this book, "IBH" emphasizes learning how to **improvise** your own solos more than how to play "classic" licks or solos (as in this book). The 64 page Volume I book/90 min. tape (for C harp) is $12.95.

Volume II (for key of A harp) is for intermediate players who understand blues scales and structures. The first half of Vol. II will be easy for anyone who has read this book (BRME), the second half uses lots of bending in its blues and rock solos. Volume II (book/90 min. tape) is also $12.95.

Bending The Blues

This 64 page book and 90 minute cassette covers *everything* you'll ever need to know about **bending,** the technique of using your tongue to make a note sound **lower** and **wail-ier** than it should. From getting that first feeble bend, to using easy 2, 4, 5, and 6 in bends, to full pro-level techniques! Use with A, C, or F ten hole harps. The American Harmonica Newsletter called this: "...THE most important book and cassette on blues harp!" Book $4.95, book and 90 minute cassette $12.95.

Harmonica Positions

"Positions" refers to the fact that the **blues scale** can be played in **five different ways** (or positions) on the harp. Most of what's in *this* book (BRME) is in second, or **"cross,"** position. But the other four positions are fun, too, and this package explains each position for beginner, intermediate, and pro level players. Lots of playalong music, for key of "A" harmonica. Book $4.95. 90 minute tape only $9.95.

How To Play C & W Harmonica

Like Country & Western (C & W) music? This 64 page book and 90 minute cassette will have you playing country licks, riffs and solos in the styles of **Charlie McCoy** and **Mickey Raphael,** almost instantly. Only $4.95 (book only) or $12.95 (book & 90 min. cassette, for key of C harmonica).

Instant Blues/Jazz Chromatic Harp

This 112 page book and 90 minute tape starts off with **Little Walter** blues style, then goes on to the more complex styles of **Stevie Wonder** and **Toots Thielemans** — you'll be amazed at how easy it is! Book & cassette only $18.95, call for a great deal on a "chro," if you need one.

Music Theory Made Easy!

Lots of us harp players don't know much theory, but I'll teach you enough to compose your own songs, understand chords and scales, read blues and jazz chord charts, and: **Not feel nervous when jamming with others!** 80 page book $5.95, 90 min. tape $9.95, and: **You don't need to read music!**

Rhythm Help! Instant Guitar! Kid's Harp! Songbook!

Instant Guitar — a book, 90 minute cassette and the "Chord-Snaffle." Play within minutes (beginners only), $12.95.
Instant Rhythm Kit — improve your rhythm & play harp better: Book, cassette, and drumsticks a great deal at $9.95!
Kid's harp method (ages 4-9): Book/tape **or** video just $9.95. Harps hard to find? Hohner Big River A or Bb $13. *Any* harp available. Teachers! Call for volume discounts!
NEW: The Pocket Harmonica Songbook! Over 40 songs for beginning/intermediate players, 64 pages only $4.95!

David Harp's musical i press
P.O. Box 1561-BR, Montpelier, Vermont 05602
Phone Orders* call (802) 223-1544 (Fax: 223-0543)
Visa, Mastercharge, and AmEx Cards Welcome*

To order: Call in your order or send a check or money order. Please clearly identify the items you want, and include the following shipping charges. We ship via UPS Ground unless otherwise instructed. **U.S. Orders:** Please add $4 for first item, plus $1 for each additional item. **Canadian Orders:** Please add $6 first item, $2 each add'l item. **Other Foreign Orders:** we'll charge your Visa/MC/AmEx what it costs us, or call/fax/write in advance for charges.

* Know Exactly what you want and have a Credit Card?
Call our **AUTOMATED ORDER LINE: (800) MOJO-IS-I**
(665-6474)